What We Wear When We Take Care

Sarah Finan

Candlewick Press

Sometimes we wear helmets to protect our heads in case things

clatter,

clonk,

bump,

or crash!

Sometimes we wear headphones to protect our ears from sounds that

boom,

rumble,

Sometimes we wear goggles to protect our eyes from things that

fizz,

splish,

or

splash.

Sometimes we wear masks to protect from germs when we

ahhh,

achoo,
cough,

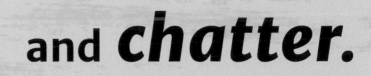

and **chatter.**

Sometimes we wear vests to help us
to be seen as trains, trucks, and cars

zoom, **whoosh,**

honk,
screech,

and **stop** for us.

Sometimes we wear gloves
to protect our hands when
touching things that

scratch,

claw,

freeze,

or **splatter!**

Sometimes we need
boots to protect our feet
in case things

slip,

drip-
drop,

or
squelch.

There is a lot of safety equipment
we can wear when we take care,
from our heads to our toes.

What do YOU wear to take care?

**In loving memory of my brilliant builder dad,
John Michael Finan. Thank you for being the best.**

First edition 2024

Library of Congress Catalog Card Number pending
ISBN 978-1-5362-2770-3

24 25 26 27 28 29 CCP 10 9 8 7 6 5 4 3 2 1

Printed in Shenzhen, Guangdong, China

This book was typeset in Merriweather Sans.
The illustrations were hand-painted and colored digitally.

Candlewick Press
99 Dover Street
Somerville, Massachusetts 02144

www.candlewick.com